The Compleat Cook

By

Hannah Woolley

The Compleat Cook

To Bake Red Deere.

Parboyl it, and then sauce it in Vinegar then Lard it very thick, and season it with Pepper, Ginger and Nutmegs, put it into a deep Pye with good store of sweet butter, and let it bake, when it is baked, take a pint of Hippocras, halfe a pound of sweet butter, two or three Nutmeg, little Vinegar, poure it into the Pye in the Oven and let it lye and soake an hour, then take it out, and when it is cold stop the vent hole.

To make fine Pancakes fryed without Butter or Lard.

Take a pint of Cream, and six new laid Egs, beat them very well together, put in a quarter of a pound of Sugar, and one Nutmeg or a little beaten Mace (which you please) and so much flower as will thicken almost as much as ordinarily Pancake batter; your Pan must be heated reasonably hot & wiped with a clean Cloth, this done put in your Batter as thick or thin as you please.

To dresse a Pig the French manner.

Take it and spit it, & lay it down to the fire, and when your Pig is through warme, skin her, and cut her off the Spit as another Pig is, and so divide it in twenty peeces more or lesse as you please; when you have so done, take some White-wine and strong broth, and stew it therein, with an Onion or two mixed very small, a little Time also minced with Nutmeg sliced and grated Pepper, some Anchoves and Elder Vinegar, and a very little sweet Butter, and Gravy if you have it, so Dish it up with the same Liquor it is stewed in, with French Bread sliced under it, with Oranges and Lemons.

To make a Steake pye, with a French Pudding in the Pye.

Season your Steaks with Pepper & Nutmegs, and let it stand an hour in a Tray then take a piece of the leanest of a Legg of Mutton and mince it small with Suet and a few sweet herbs, tops of young Time, a branch of Pennyroyal, two or three of red Sage, grated bread, yolks of Eggs, sweet Cream, Raisins of the Sun; work altogether like a Pudding, with your hand stiff, and roul them round like Bals, and put them into the Steaks in a deep Coffin, with a piece of sweet Butter; sprinkle a little Verjuyce on it, bake it, then cut it up and roul Sage leaves and fry them, and stick them upright in the wals, and serve your Pye without a Cover, with the juyce of an Orange or Lemon.

An excellent way of dressing Fish.

Take a piece of fresh Salmon, and wash it clean in a little Vinegar and water, and let it lie a while in it, then put it into a great Pipkin with a cover, and put to it some six spoonfuls of water and four of Vinegar, and as much of white-wine, a good deal of Salt a handful of sweet herbs, a little white Sorrel, a few Cloves, a little stick of Cinamon, a little Mace; put all these in a Pipkin close, and set it in a Kettle of seething water, and there let it stew three hours.

You may do Carps, Eeles, Trouts, &c. this way, and they Tast also to your mind.

To fricate Sheeps-feet.

Take Sheeps-feet, slit the bone, and pick them very clean, then put them in a Frying-pan, with a Ladlefull of strong Broth, a piece of Butter, and a little Salt, after they have fryed a while, put to them a little Parsley, green Chibals, a little young Speremint and Tyme, all shred very small, and a little beaten Pepper; when you think they are fryed almost enough, have a lear made for them with the yolks of two or three Eggs, some Gravy of Mutton, a little Nutmegg, and juyce of a Lemon wrung therein, and put this lear to the Sheeps feet as they fry in the Pan, then toss them once or twice, and put them forth into the Dish you mean to serve them in.

To fricate Calves Chaldrons.

Take a Calves Chaldron, after it is little more then half boyled, and when it is cold, cut it into little bits as big as Walnuts; season it with beaten Cloves, Salt, Nutmeg, Mace, and a little Pepper, an Onion, Parsley, and a little Tarragon, all shred very small, then put it into a frying-pan, with a Ladlefull of strong broth, and a little piece of sweet Butter, so fry it; when it is fryed enough, have a little lear made with the Gravy of Mutton, the juyce of a Lemon and Orange, the yolks of three or four Eggs, and a little Nutmeg grated therein; put all this to your Chaldrons in the Pan, Toss your Fricat two or three times, then dish it, and so serve it up.

To Fricate Champigneons.

Make ready your champigneons as you do for stewing, and when you have poured away the black liquor that comes from them, put your champigneons into a Frying pan with a piece of sweet Butter, a little Parsley, Tyme, sweet Marjoram, a piece of Onion shred very small, a little Salt and fine beaten Pepper, so fry them till they be enough, so have ready the lear abovesaid, and put it to the champigneons whilst they are in the Pan, toss them two or three times, put them forth and serve them.

To make buttered Loaves.

Take the yolks of twelve Eggs, and six whites, and a quarter of a pint of yeast, when you have beaten the Eggs well, strain them with the yeast into a Dish, then put to it a little Salt, and two rases of Ginger beaten very small, then put flower to it till it come to a high Past that will not cleave, then you must roule it upon your hands and afterwards put it into a warm Cloath and let it lye there a quarter of an hour, then make it up in little Loaves, bake; against it is baked prepare a pound and a half of Butter, a quarter of a pint of white wine, and halfe a pound of Sugar; This being melted and beaten together with it, set them into the Oven a quarter of an hour.

To murine Carps, Mullet, Gurnet, Rochet, or Wale, &c.

Take a quart of water to a Gallon of Vinegar, a good handful of Bayleaves, as much Rosemary, a quarter of a pound of Pepper beaten; put all these together, and let it seeth softly, and season it with a little Salt, then fry your Fish with frying Oyle till it be enough, then put in an earthen Vessell, and lay the Bayleaves and Rosemary between and about the Fish, and pour the Broth upon it, and when it is cold, cover it, *&c.*

To make a Calves Chaldron Pye.

Take a Calves Chaldron, half boyl it, and cool it; when it is cold mince it as small as grated bread, with halfe a pound of Marrow; season it with Salt, beaten Cloves, Mace, Nutmeg a little Onion, and some of the outmost rind of a Lemon minced very small, and wring in the juyce of halfe a Lemon, and then mix all together, then make a piece of puff Past, and lay a leaf therof in a silver Dish of the bigness to contain the meat, then put in your meat, and cover it with another leaf of the same Past, and bake it; and when it is baked take it out, and open it, and put in the juyce of two or three Oranges, stir it well together, then cover it againe and serve it. Be sure none of your Orange kernels be among your Pye-meat.

To make a Pudding of a Calves Chaldron.

Take your Chaldron after it is half boyled and cold, mince it as small as you can with half a pound of Beef Suet, or as much Marrow, season it with a little Onion, Parsley, Tyme, and the outmost rind of a piece of Lemon, all shred very small, Salt, beaten Nutmeg, Cloves and mace mixed together, with the yolks of four or five Eggs, and a little sweet Cream; then have ready the great Gutts of a Mutton scraped and washed very clean; let your Gutt have lain in white-wine and Salt halfe a day before you use it; when your meat is mixed and made up somewhat stiff put it into the Sheeps-gutt, and so boyl it, when it is boyled enough, serve it to the Table in the Gutt.

To make a Banbury Cake.

Take a peck of pure Wheat-flower, six pound of Currans, half a pound of Sugar, two pound of Butter, halfe an ounce of Cloves and Mace, a pint and a halfe of Ale-yeast, and a little Rosewater; then boyle as much new-milk as will serve to knead it, and when it is almost cold, put into it as much Sack as will thicken it, and so work it all together before a fire, pulling it two or three times in pieces, after make it up.

To make a Devonshire White-pot.

Take a pint of Cream and straine four Eggs into it, and put a little Salt and a little sliced Nutmeg, and season it with Sugar somewhat sweet; then take almost a penny Loaf of fine bread sliced very thin, and put it into a Dish that will hold it, the Cream and the Eggs being put to it; then take a handfull of Raisins of the Sun being boyled, and a little sweet Butter, so bake it.

To make Rice Cream.

Take a quart of Cream, two good handfuls of Rice-flower, a quarter of a pound of Sugar and flower beaten very small, mingle your Sugar and flower together, put it into your Cream, take the yolk of an Egg, beat it with a spoonfull or two of Rosewater, then put it to the Cream, and stir all these together, and set it over a quick fire, keeping it continually stirring till it be as thick as water-pap.

To make a very Good Great Oxfordshire Cake.

Take a peck of flower by weight, and dry it a little, & a pound and a halfe of Sugar, one ounce of Cinamon, half an ounce of Nutmegs, a quarter of an ounce of Mace and Cloves, a good spoonfull of Salt, beat your Salt and Spice very fine, and searce it, and mix it with your flower and Sugar; then take three pound of butter and work it in the flower, it will take three hours working; then take a quart of Ale-yeast, two quarts of Cream, half a pint of Sack, six grains of Ambergreece dissolved in it, halfe a pint of Rosewater, sixteen Eggs, eight of the Whites, mix these with the flower, and knead them well together, then let it lie warm by your fire till your Oven be hot, which must be little hotter then for manchet; when you make it ready for your Oven, put to your Cake six pound of Currans, two pound of Raisins, of the Sun stoned and minced, so make up your Cake, and set it in your oven stopped close; it wil take three houres a baking; when baked, take it out and frost it over with the white of an Egge and Rosewater, well beat together, and strew fine Sugar upon it, and then set it again into the Oven, that it may Ice.

To make a Pumpion Pye.

Take about halfe a pound of Pumpion and slice it, a handfull of Tyme, a little Rosemary, Parsley and sweet Marjoram slipped off the stalks, and chop them smal, then take Cinamon, Nutmeg, Pepper, and six Cloves, and beat them; take ten Eggs and beat them; then mix them, and beat them altogether, and put in as much Sugar as you think fit, then fry them like a froiz; after it is fryed, let it stand till it be cold, then fill your Pye, take sliced Apples thinne round wayes, and lay a row of the Froiz, and a layer of Apples with Currans betwixt the layer while your Pye is fitted, and put in a good deal of sweet butter before you close it; when the Pye is baked, take six yolks of Eggs, some white-wine or Verjuyce, & make a Caudle of this, but not too thick; cut up the Lid and put it in, stir them well together whilst the Eggs and Pumpions be not perceived, and so serve it up.

To make the best Sausages that ever was eat.

Take a leg of young Pork, and cut of all the lean, and shred it very small, but leave none of the strings or skins amongst it, then take two pound of Beef Suet, and shred it small, then take two handfuls of red Sage, a little Pepper and Salt, and Nutmeg, and a small piece of an Onion, chop them altogether with the flesh and Suet; if it is small enough, put the yolk of two or three Eggs and mix altogether, and make it up in a Past if you will use it, roul out as many pieces as you please in the form of an ordinary Sausage, and so fry them, this Past will keep a fortnight upon occasion.

To boyle a Fresh Fish.

Take a Carp, or other, & put them into a deep Dish, with a pint of white-wine, a large Mace, a little Tyme, Rosemary, a piece of sweet Butter, and let him boyle between two dishes in his owne blood, season it with Pepper and Verjuyce, and so serve it up on Sippets.

To make Fritters.

Take halfe a pint of Sack, a pint of Ale, some Ale-yeast, nine Eggs, yolks and whites, beat them very well, the Egg first, then altogether, put in some Ginger, and Salt, and fine flower, then let it stand an houre or two; then shred in the Apples; when you are ready to fry them, your suet must be all Beef-suet, or halfe Beef, and halfe Hoggs-suet tryed out of the leafe.

To make Loaves of Cheese-Curds.

Take a Porringer full of Curds, and four Eggs, whites, and yolks, and so much flower as will make it stiff, then take a little Ginger, Nutmeg, & some Salt, make them into loaves and set them into an oven with a quick heat; when they begin to change Colour take them out, and put melted Butter to them, and some Sack, and good store of Sugar, and so serve it.

To make fine Pies after the French fashion.

Take a pound and half of Veale, two pound of suet, two pound of great Raisins stoned, half a pound of Prunes, as much of Currans, six Dates, two Nutmegs, a spoonfull of Pepper, an ounce of Sugar, an ounce of Carrawayes, a Saucer of Verjuyce, and as much Rosewater, this will make three fair Pyes, with two quarts of flower, three yolks of Egges, and halfe a pound of Butter.

A Singular Receit for making a Cake.

Take halfe a peck of flower, two pound of Butter, mingle it with the flower, three Nutmegs, & a little Mace, Cinamon, Ginger, halfe a pound of Sugar, leave some out to strew on the top, mingle these well with the flower and Butter, five pound of Currans well washed, and pickt, and dryed in a warm Cloth, a wine pint of Ale yeast, six Eggs, leave out the whites, a quart of Cream boyled and almost cold againe: work it well together and let it be very lith, lay it in a warm Cloth, and let it lye half an hour against the fire. Then make it up with the white of an Egg, a little Butter, Rosewater and Sugar; Ice it over and put it into the Oven, and let it stand one whole hour and a half.

To make a great Curd Loaf.

Take the Curds of three quarts of new milk clean whayed, and rub into them a little of the finest flower you can get, then take half a race of Ginger, and slice it very thin, and put it into your Curds with a little Salt, then take halfe a pint of good Ale Yeast and put to it, then take ten Eggs, but three of the Whites, let there be so much flower as will make it into a reasonable stiff Past, then put it into an indifferant hot cloth, and lay it before the fire to rise while your Oven is heating, then make it up into a Loaf, and when it is baked, cut up the top of the Loaf, and put in a pound and a half of melted Butter, and a good deale of Sugar in it.

To make buttered Loaves of Cheese-curds.

Take three quarts of new Milk, and put in as much Rennet as will turn, take your Whay clean away, then breake your Curds very small with your hands, and put in six yolks of Eggs, but one white; an handfull of grated bread, an handfull of Flower, a little Salt mingled altogether; work it with your hand, roul it into little Loaves, then set them in a Pan buttered, then beat the yolk of an Egg with a little Beer, and wipe them over with a feather, then set them in the Oven as for Manchet, and stop that close three quarters of an hour, then take halfe a pound of butter three spoonfuls of water, a Nutmeg sliced thin, a little Sugar, set it on the fire, stir it till it be thick; when your Loaves are baked, cut off the tops and butter them with this Butter, some under, some over, and strow some Sugar on them.

To make Cheese-loaves.

Grate a Wheat-Loafe, and take as much Curd as bread, to that put eight yolks of Eggs and four whites, and beat them very well, then take a little Cream but let it be very thick, put altogether, and make them up with two handfuls of flower, the Curds must be made of new milk and whayed very dry, you must make them like little Loaves and bake them in an Oven; and being baked cut them up, and have in readinesse some sweet Butter, Sugar, Nutmeg sliced and mingled together, put it into the Loaves, and with it stir the Cream well together, then cover them again with the tops, and serve them with a little Sugar scraped on.

To make Puff.

Take four pints of new milke, rennet, take out all the Whay very clean, and wring it in a dry Cloth, then strain it in a wooden Dish till they become as Cream, then take the yolks of two Egges, and beat them and put them to the Curds, and leave them with the Curds, then put a spoonfull of Cream to them, and if you please halfe a spoonfull of Rosewater, and as much flower beat in it as will make it of an indifferent stiffnesse, just to roul on a Plate, then take off the Kidney of Mutton suet and purifie it, and fry them in it, and serve them with Butter, Rosewater and Sugar.

To make Elder Vinegar.

Gather the flowers of Elder, pick them very clean, and dry them in the Sun on a gentle heat, and take to every quart of Vinegar a good handfull of flowers and let it stand to Sun a fortnight, then strain the Vinegar from the flowers, and put it into the barrell againe, and when you draw a quart of Vinegar, draw a quart of water, and put it into the Barrell luke warme.

To make good Vinegar.

Take one strike of Malt, and one of Rye ground, and mash them together, and take (if they be good) three pound of Hops, if not four pound; make two Hogs-heads of the best of that Malt and Rye, then lay the Hogs-head where the Sunne may have power over them, and when it is ready to Tun, fill your hogs-heads where they lye, then let them purge cleer and cover them with two flate stones, and within a week after when you bake, take two wheat loaves hot out of the Oven, and put into each hogs-head a loaf, you must use this foure times, you must brew this in *Aprill*, and let it stand till *June*, then draw them clearer, then wash the Hogs-heads cleane, and put the beer in again; if you will have it Rose-vinegar, you must put in a strike and a half of Roses; if Elder-vinegar, a peck of the flowers; if you will have it white, put no thing in it after it is drawn, and so let it stand till *Michaelmas*; if you will have it coloured red, take four gallons of strong Ale as you can get, and Elder berries picked a few full clear, and put them in your pan with the Ale, set them ouer the fire till you guesse that a pottle is wasted, then take if off the fire, and let it stand till it be store cold, and the next day strain it into the Hogs-head, then lay them in a Cellar or buttery which you please.

To make a Coller of Beef.

Take the thinnest end of a coast of beef, boyl it and lay it in Pump-water, and a little salt, three dayes shifting it once every day, and the last day put a pint of Claret Wine to it, and when you take it out of the water, let it lye two or three hours a drayning, then cut it almost to the end in three slices, then bruise a little Cochinell and a very little Allum, and mingle it with the Claret-wine, and colour the meat all over with it, then take a dozen of Anchoves, wash them and bone them, and lay them into the Beef, and season it with Cloves, Mace, and Pepper, and two handfuls of salt, and a little sweet Marjoram and Tyme, and when you make it up, roul the innermost slice first, and the other two upon it, being very wel seasoned every where, and bind it hard with Tape, then put it into a stone-pot, something bigger then the Coller, and pour upon it a pint of Claret-wine, and halfe a pint of wine-vinegar, a sprig of Rosemary, and a few Bayleave and bake it very well; before it is quite cold, take it out of the Pot, and you may keep it dry as long as you please.

To make an Almond Pudding.

Take two or three French-Rowles, or white penny bread, cut them in slices, and put to the bread as much Cream as wil cover it, put it on the fire till your Cream and bread be very warm, then take a ladle or spoon and beat it very well together, put to this twelve Eggs, but not above foure whites, put in Beef Suet, or Marrow, according to your discretion, put a pretty quantity of Currans and Raisins, season the Pudding with Nutmeg, Mace, Salt, and Sugar, but very little flower for it will make it sad and heavy; make a piece of puff past as much as will cover your dish, so cut it very handsomely what fashion you please; Butter the bottome of your Dish, put the pudding into the Dish, set it in a quick Oven, not too hot as to burne it, let it bake till you think it be enough, scrape on Sugar and serve it up.

To boyle Cream with French Barly.

Take the third part of a pound of French Barley, wash it well with fair water, and let it lie all night in fair water, in the morning set two skillets on the fire with faire water, and in one of them put your Barley, and let it boyle till the water look red, then put the water from it, and put the Barley into the other warme water, thus boyl it and change with fresh warm water till it boyl white, then strain the water clean from it, then take a quart of Creame, put into it a Nutmeg or two quartered, a little large Mace and some Sugar, and let it boyl together a quarter of an hour, and when it hath thus boyled put into it the yolks of three or foure Eggs, well beaten with a little Rosewater, then dish it forth, and eat it cold.

To make Cheese-Cakes.

Take three Eggs and beat them very well, and as you beat them, put to them as much fine flower as will make them thick, then put to them three or four Eggs more, and beat them altogether; then take one quart of Creame, and put into it a quarter of a pound of sweet butter, and set them over the fire, and when it begins to boyle, put to it your Eggs and flower, stir it very well, and let it boyle till it be thick, then season it with Salt, Cinamon, Sugar, and Currans, and bake it.

To make a Quaking Pudding.

Take a pint and somewhat more of thick Creame, ten Egges, put the whites of three, beat them very well with two spoonfuls of Rosewater; mingle with your Creame three spoonfuls of fine flower, mingle it so well, that there be no lumps in it, put it altogether, and season it according to your Tast; Butter a Cloth very well, and let it be thick that it may not run out, and let it boyle for half an hour as fast as you can, then take it up and make Sauce with Butter, Rosewater and Sugar, and serve it up.

You may stick some blanched Almonds upon it if you please.

To Pickle Cucumbers.

Put them in an Earthen Vessel, lay first a Lay of Salt and Dill, then a Lay of Cucumbers, and so till they be all Layed, put in some Mace and whole pepper, and some Fennel-seed according to direction, then fill it up with Beer-Vinegar, and a clean board and a stone upon it to keepe them within the pickle, and so keep them close covered, and if the Vinegar is black, change them into fresh.

To Pickle Broom Buds.

Take your Buds before they be yellow on the top, make a brine of Vinegar and Salt, which you must do onely by shaking it together till the Salt be melted, then put in your Buds, and keepe stirred once in a day till they be sunk within the Vinegar, be sure to keep close covered.

To keep Quinces raw all the year.

Take some of the worst Quinces and cut them into small pieces, and Coares and Parings, boyle them in water, and put to a Gallon of water, some three spoonfuls of Salt, as much Honey; boyle these together till they are very strong, and when it is cold, put it into half a pint of Vinegar in a wooden

Vessell or Earthen Pot; and take then as many of your best Quinces as will go into your Liquor, then stop them up very close that no Aire get into them, and they will keep all the yeare.

To make a Gooseberry Foole.

Take your Gooseberries, and put them in a Silver or Earthen Pot, and set it in a Skillet of boyling Water, and when they are coddled enough strain them, then make them hot again, when they are scalding hot, beat them very well with a good piece of fresh butter, Rosewater and Sugar, and put in the yolke of two or three Eggs; you may put Rosewater into them, and so stir it altogether, and serve it to the Table when it is cold.

To make an Otemeale Pudding.

Take a Porringer full of Oatmeale beaten to flower, a pint of Creame, one Nutmeg, four Eggs beaten, three whites, a quarter of a pound of Sugar, a pound of Beefe-suet well minced, mingle all these together and so bake it. An houre will bake it.

To make a green Pudding.

Take a penny loafe of stale Bread, grate it, put to halfe a pound of Sugar, grated Nutmeg, as much Salt as will season it, three quarters of a pound of beef-suet shred very small, then take sweet Herbs, the most of them Marigolds, eight Spinages: shred the Herbs very small, mix all well together, then take two Eggs and work them up together with your hand, and make them into round balls, and when the water boyles put them in, serve them with Rosewater, Sugar, and Butter or Sauce.

To make good Sausages.

Take the lean of a Legge of Pork, and four pound of Beefe-suet, or rather butter, shred them together very small, then season it with three quarters of an ounce of Pepper, and halfe an ounce of Cloves and Mace mixed together, as the Pepper is, a handfull of Sage when it is chopt small, and as much salt as you thinke will make them tast well of it; mingle all these with the meat, then break in ten Eggs, all but two or three of the whites, then temper it all well with your hands, and fill it into Hoggs gutts, which you must have ready for them; you must tye the ends of them like Puddings, and when you eat them you must boyle them on a soft fire; a hot will crack the skins, and the goodnesse boyle out of them.

To make Toasts.

Cut two penny Loaves in round slices and dip them in half a pint of Cream or cold water, then lay them abroad in a Dish, and beat three Eggs and grated Nutmegs, and Sugar, beat them with the Cream, then take your frying Pan and melt some butter in it, and wet one side of your Toasts and lay them in on the wet side, then pour in the rest upon them, and so fry them; send them in with Rosewater, butter and sugar.

Spanish Cream.

Put hot water in a bucket and go with it to the Milking, then poure out the Water, and instantly milke into it, and presently strain it into milk-Pans of an ordinary fulnesse, but not after an ordinary way for you must set your Pan on the ground and stand on a stool, and pour it forth that it may rise in bubbles with the fall; this on the morrow will be a very tough Cream, which you must take off with your Skimmer, and lay it in the Dish, laying upon laying; and if you please strew some sugar between them.

To make Clouted Cream.

Take foure quarts of Milke, one of Cream, six spoonfuls of Rosewater, put these together in a great Earthen Milke-Pan, & set it upon a fire of Charcoale well kindled, you must be sure the fire be not too hot; then let it stand a day and a night; and when you go to take it off, loose the edge of your Cream around about with a Knife, then take your board, and lay the edges that is left beside the board, cut into many pieces, and put them into the Dish first, and scrape some fine Sugar upon them, then take your board and take off your Cream as clean from the Milk as you can, and lay it upon your Dish, and if your Dish be little, there will be some left, the which you may put into what fashion you please, and scrape good store of Sugar upon it.

A good Cream

When you Churn Butter, take out six spoonfuls of Cream, just as it is to turne to Butter, that is, when it is a little frothy; then boyle good Cream as must as will make a Dish, and season it with Sugar, and a little Rosewater; when it is quite cold enough, mingle it very well with that you take out of the Churn, and so Dish it.

To make Piramidis Cream.

Take a quart of water, and six ounces of harts horn, and put it into a Bottle with Gum-dragon, and Gum-arabick, of each as much as a small Nut, put all this into the Bottle, which must be so big as will hold a pint more; for if it be full it will break; stop it very Close with a Cork, and tye a Cloth about it, put the Bottle into a pot of beef when it is boyling, and let it boyle three hours, then take as much Cream as there is Jelly, and halfe a pound of Almonds well beaten with Rosewater, so that you cannot discern what they be, mingle the Cream and the Almonds together, then strain it, and do so two or three times to get all you can out of the Almonds, then put jelly when it is cold into a silver Bason, and the Cream to it; sweeten it as you like, put in two or three grains of Musk and Ambergreece, set it over the fire, stirring it continually and skimming it, till it be seething hot, but let it not boyle, then put it into an old fashion drinking-Glasse, and let it stand till it is cold, and when you will use it, hold your Glass in a warm hand, and loosen it with a Knife, and whelm it into a Dish, and have in readinesse Pine Apple blown, and stick it all over, and serve it in with Cream or without as you please.

To make a Sack Cream.

Set a quart of Cream on the fire, when it is boyled, drop in a spoonfull of sack, and stir it well the while, that it curd not, so do till you have dropped in six spoonfuls, then season it with sugar, Nutmeg, and strong water.

To boyle Pigeons.

Stuffe the Pigeons with Parsley, and butter, and put them into an Earthen Pot, and put some sweet butter to them and let them boyle; take Parsley, Tyme, and Rosemary, chop them and put them to them; take some sweet butter, and put in withall some spinage, take a little gross Pepper and Salt, and season it withall, then take the yolk of an Egge and strain it with Verjuyce, and put to them, lay sippets in the Dish and serve it.

To make an Apple-Tansey.

Pare your Apples and cut them in thin round slices, then fry them in good sweet Butter, then take ten Eggs, sweet Cream, Nutmeg, Cinamon, Ginger, Sugar, with a little Rosewater, beat all these together, and poure it upon your Apples and fry it.

The French-Barly-Cream.

Take a quart of Cream, and boyle in a Porrenger of French-Barley, that hath been boyled in a nine waters, put in some large Mace and a little Cinamon, boyling it a quarter of an hour; then take two quarts of Almonds blanched, and beat it very small with Rosewater, or Orange-water, and some Sugar; and the Almonds being strained into the Liquor, put it over the fire, stirring it till it be ready to boyle; then take it off the fire, stirring it till it be halfe cold; then put to it two spoonfuls of Sack or White-Wine, and when it is cold, serve it in, remembring to put in some Salt.

To make a Chicken or Pigeon-Pye.

Take your Pigeons (if they be not very young) cut them into four quarters, one sweetbread sliced the long way, that it may be thin, and the pieces not too big, one Sheeps tongue, little more then parboyl'd, and the skin puld off, and the tongue cut in slices, two or three slices of Veale, as much of Mutton, young chicken (if not little) quarter them, Chick-heads, Lark, or any such like, Pullets, Coxcombs, Oysters, Calves-Udder cut in pieces, good store of Marrow for seasoning, take as much Pepper and Salt as you think fit to season it slightly; good store of sweet Marjoram, a little Time and Lemon-Pill fine sliced; season it well with these Spices as the time of the year will afford; put in either of Chesnuts (if you put in Chesnuts they must first be either boyl'd or roasted) Gooseberries or Guage, large Mace will do well in this Pye, then take a little piece of Veale parboyl'd and slice it very fine, as much Marrow as meat stirred amongst it, then take grated Bread, as much as a quarter of the meat, four yolks of Eggs or more according to the stuffe you make, shred Dates as small as may be, season it with salt, but not too salt. Nutmeg as much as will season it, sweet Marjoram pretty store very small shred, work it up with as much sweet Creame as will make it up in little Puddings, some long, some round, so put as many of them in the Pye as you please; put therein two or three spoonfulls of Gravy of Mutton, or so much strong Mutton broth before you put it in the Oven, the bottome of boyled Artichokes, minced Marrow over and in the bottom of the Pye after your Pye is baked; when you put it up, have some five yolks of Eggs minced, and the juyce of two or three Oranges, the meat of one Lemon cut in pieces, a little White and Claret

Wine; put this in your Pye being well mingled, and shake it very well together.

To boyle a Capon or Hen.

Take a young Capon or Hen, when you draw them, take out the fall of the Leafe clean away, and being well washed, fill the belly with Oysters; prepare some Mutton, the neck, but boyle it in smal peices and skim it well, then put your Capon into the Pipkin, and when it is boyled, skim it again; be sure you have no more water then will cover your meat, then put it into a pint of white wine, some Mace, two or three Cloves and whole Pepper; a quarter of an hour before your meat be boyled enough, put into the Pipkin, three Anchoves stript from the Bones and washed, and be sure you put Salt at the first to your meat; a little Parsley Spinage, Endive, Sorrell, Rosemary, or such kind of Herbs will do well to boyle with the Broth, and being ready to Dish it, having sippets cut then take the Oysters out of the Capon, and lay them in the Dish with the Broth, and put some juyce of Lemons and Orange into it according to your taste.

To make Balls of Veale.

Take the Lean of a Leg of Veal, and cut out the Sinews, mince it very small, and with it some fat of Beef suet; if the Leg of Veal be of a Cow Calfe, the Udder will be good instead of Beef suet; when it is very well beaten together with the mincing Knife, have some Cloves, Mace, and Pepper beaten, and with Salt season your meat, putting in some Vinegar, then make up your meat into little Balls, and having very good strong Broth made of Mutton, set your Balls to boyle in it; when they are boyled enough, take the yolks of five or six Eggs well beaten with as much Vinegar as you please to like, and some of the Broth mingled together, stir it into all your Balls and Broth, give it a waume on the fire, then Dish up the Balls upon Sippits and pour the sauce on it.

To make Mrs. Shellyes *Cake.*

Take a peck of fine flower, and three pound of the best Butter, work your flower and butter very well together, then take ten Eggs, leave out six whites, a pint and a halfe of Ale-yeast: beat the Eggs and yeast together, and put them to the flower; take six pound of blanched Almonds, beat them very well, putting in sometime Rosewater to keepe them from Oyling; adde what spice you please; let this be put to the rest, with a quarter of a pint of Sack, and a little saffron; and when you have made all this into Past, cover it warme before the fire, and let it rise for halfe an hour, then put in twelve pound of Currans well washed and dryed, two pound of Raisins of the Sun stoned and cut small, one pound of Sugar; the sooner you put it into the Oven after the fruit is put in, the better.

To make Almond Jumballs.

Take a pound of Almonds to halfe a pound of double refined Sugar beaten and Searced, lay your Almonds in water a day before you blanch them, and beat them small with your Sugar; and when it is beat very small, put in a handfull of Gum-dragon, it being before over night steeped in Rosewater, and halfe a white of an Egge beaten to froth, and halfe a spoonfull of Coriander-seed as many Fennell and Aniseeds, mingle these together very well, set them upon a soft fire till it grow pretty thick, then take it off the fire, and lay it upon a clean Paper, and beat it well with a rowling pin till it work like a soft past, and so make them up, and lay them upon Papers oyld with Oyle of Almonds, then put them in your Oven, and so soon as they be throughly risen, take them out before they grow hard.

To make Cracknels.

Take halfe a pound of fine flower, dryed and searced, as much fine sugar searced, mingled with a spoonfull of Coriander-seed bruised, halfe a quarter of a pound of butter rubbed in the flower and sugar, then wet it with the yolks of two Eggs, and halfe a spoonfull of white Rosewater, a spoonfull or little more of Cream as will wet it; knead the Past till it be soft and limber to rowle well, then rowle it extreame thin, and cut them round by little plates; lay them up on buttered papers, and when they goe into the Oven, prick them, and wash the Top with the yolk of an Egg beaten, and made thin with Rosewater or faire water; they will give with keeping, therefore before they are eaten, they must be dryed in a warme Oven to make them crisp.

To Pickle Oysters.

Take Oysters and wash them cleane in their own Liquor, and let them settle, then strain it, and put your Oysters to it with a little Mace and whole pepper, as much Salt as you please, and a little Wine-Vinegar, then set them over the fire, and let them boyle leisurely till they are pretty tender; be sure to skim them still as the skim riseth; when they are enough, take them out till the Pickle be cold, then put them into any pot that will lye close, they will keep best in Caper barrels, they will keep very well six weeks.

To boyle Cream with Codlings.

Take a quart of Cream and boyle it with some Mace and Sugar, and take two yolks of Eggs, and beat them well with a spoonfull of Rosewater and a grain of Ambergreece, then put it into the Cream with a piece of sweet Butter as big as a Wall-nut, and stir it together over the fire untill it be ready to boyle, then set it some time to coole, stirring it continually till it be cold; then take a quarter of a pound of Codlings strained, and put them into a silver Dish over a few coales till they be almost dry, and being cold, and the Cream also, poure the Cream upon them, and let them stand on a soft fire covered an hour, then serve them in.

To make the Lady Albergaveres Cheese.

To one Cheese take a Gallon of new Milk, and a pint of good Cream, and mix them well together, then take a Skillet of hot water as much as will make it hotter then it comes from the Cow, then put in a spoonfull of Rennet, and stir it well together and cover it, and when it is come, take a wet Cloth and lay it on your Cheese-Mot, and take up the Curd and not break it; and put it into your Mot; and when your Mot is full, lay on the Suiker, and every two hours turn your Cheese in wet Cloathes wrung dry; and lay on a little more wet, at night take as much salt as you can between your finger and thumb, and salt your Cheese on both sides; let them lye in Presses all night in a wet Cloth; the next day lay them on a Table between a dry Cloth, the next day lay them in Grasse, and every other day change your Grasse, they will be ready to eat in nine dayes; if you will have them ready sooner, cover them with a Blanket.

To dresse Snayles.

Take your Snayles (they are no way so as in Pottage) and wash them well in many waters, and when you have done put them in a white Earthen Pan, or a very wide Dish, and put as much water to them as will cover them, and then set your Dish or Pan on some coales, that it may heat by little and little, and then the Snayles will come out of the shells and so dye, and being dead, take them out, and wash them very well in Water and salt twice or thrice over; then put them in a Pipkin with Water and Salt, and let them boyle a little while in that, so take away the rude slime they have, then take them out againe and put them in a Cullender; then take excellent sallet Oyle and beat it a great while upon the fire in a frying Pan, and when it boyls very fast, slice two or three Onyons in it, and let them fry well, then put the Snayles in the Oyle and Onyons, and let them stew together a little, then put the Oyle, Onyons, and Snayles altogether in an earthen Pipkin of a fit size for your Snayles, and put as much warm water to them as will serve to boyle them, and make the Pottage and season them with Salt, and so let them boyle three or foure hours; then mingle Parsly, Pennyroyall, Fennell, Tyme, and such Herbs, and when they are minced put them in a Morter, and beat them as you doe for Green-sauce, and put in some crums of bread soaked in the Pottage of the Snayles, and then dissolve it all in the Morter with a little Saffron and Cloves well beaten, and put in as much Pottage into the Morter as will make the Spice and bread and Herbs like thickning for a pot, so put them all into the Snayles and let them stew in it, and when you serve them up, you may squeeze into the pottage a Lemon, and put in a little Vinegar, or if you put in a Clove of Garlick among the Herbs, and beat it with them in the Morter; it will not tast the worse; serve them up in a Dish with sippets of Bread in the bottom. The Pottage is very nourishing, and they use them that are apt to a Consumption.

To boyle a rump of Beefe after the French fashion.

Take a rump of Beef, or the little end of the Brisket, and parboyle it halfe an houre, then take it up and put it in a deep Dish, then slash it in the side that the gravy may come out, then throw a little Pepper and salt betweene every cut, then fill up the Dish with the best Claret wine, and put to it three or foure pieces of large Mace, and set it on the coales close covered, and boyle it above an houre and a halfe, but turn it often in the mean time; then with a spoon take of the fat and fill it with Claret wine, and slice six Onyons, and a handfull of Cappers or broom buds, halfe a dozen of hard Lettice sliced, three spoonfuls of wine-Vinegar and as much verjuyce, and then set it a boyling with these things in it till it be tender, and serve it up with brown Bread and Sippets fryed with butter, but be sure there be not too much fat in it when you serve it.

An excellent way of dressing Fish.

Take a piece of fresh Salmon, and wash it clean in a little Vinegar and Water, and let it lye a while in it, in a great Pipkin with a cover, and put to it six spoonfuls of Water and four of Vinegar, as much of white wine, a good deale of Salt, a bundle of sweet Herbs, a little whole Spice, a few Cloves, a little stick of Cinamon, a little Mace, take up all these in a Pipkin close, and set in a Kettle of seething Water and there let it stew three hours, You may doe Carps, Eeles, Trouts, &c. this way, alter the tast to your mind.

To make Fritters of Sheeps-feet.

Take your Sheeps feet, slit them and set them a stewing in a silver Dish, with a little strong Broth and Salt, with a stick of Cinamon, two or three Cloves, and a piece of an Orange Pill; when they are stewed, take them from the liquor and lay them upon a Pye-plate cooling; when they are cold, have some good Fritter-batter made with Sack, and dip them therein; then have ready to fry them, some excellent clarified Butter very hot in a Pan, and fry them therein; when they are fryed wring in the juyce of three or four Oranges, and toss them once or twice in a Dish, and so serve them to the Table.

To make dry Salmon Calvert in the boyling.

Take a Gallon of Water, put to it a quart of Wine or Vinegar, Verjuyce or sour Beer, and a few sweet herbs and Salt, and let your Liquor boyle extream fast, and hold your Salmon by the Tayle, and dip it in, and let it have a walme, and so dip it in and out a dozen times, and that will make your Salmon Calvert, and so boyle it till it be tender.

To make Bisket Bread.

Take a pound of Sugar searced very fine, and a pound of flower well dryed, and twelve Eggs, a handfull of Carroway-seed, six whites of Eggs, a very little Salt, beat all these together, and keep them with beating till you set them in the Oven, then put them into your Plates or Tin things, and take Butter and put into a Cloth and rub your Plate; a spoonfull into a Plate is enough, and so set them in the Oven, and let your Oven be no hotter then to bake small Pyes; if your flower be not dryed in the Oven before, they will be heavy.

To make an Almond Pudding.

Take your Almonds when they are blanched, and beat them as many as will serve for your Dish, then put to it foure or five yolks of Eggs, Rosewater, Nutmeg, Cloves and Mace, a little Sugar, and a little salt and Marrow cut into it, and so set it into the Oven, but your Oven must not be hotter then for Bisket bread; and when it is half baked, take the white of an Egg, Rosewater and fine Sugar well beaten together and very thick, and do it over with a feather, and set it in againe, then stick it over with Almonds, and so send it up.

This you may boyle in a Bag if you please, and put in a few crums of Bread into it, and eat it with butter and Sugar without Marrow.

To make an Almond Caudle.

Take three pints of Ale, boyle it with Cloves and Mace, and sliced bread in it, then have ready beaten a pound of Almonds blanched, & strain them out with a pint of White wine, and thicken the Ale with it, sweeten it if you please, and be sure you skim the Ale well when it boyles.

To make Almond bread.

Take Almonds and lay them in water all night, then blanch them and slice them, to every pound of Almonds, a pound of fine Sugar finely beaten, so mingle them together, then beat the whites of three Egs to high froth, and mix it well with the Almonds & Sugar, then have some Plates and strew some flower on them, and lay Wafers on them, and lay your Almonds with the edges upwards, lay them as round as your can, scrape a little Sugar on them, when they are ready to set in the Oven, which must not be so hot as to colour white Paper, and when they are a little baked, take them out, and them from the Plates, and set them in again, you must keepe them in a Stove.

To make Almond Cakes.

Take halfe a pound of Almonds blanched in cold water, beat them with some Rosewater till they doe not glister, then they will be beaten; if you think fit, lay seven or eight Musque Comfits dissolved in Rosewater which must not be above six or seven spoonfuls for fear of spoyling the colour; when they be thus beaten, put in half a pound of Sugar finely sifted, beat them and the Almonds together till it be well mixed, then take the whites of two Eggs, and two spoonfuls of fine flower that hath been dried in an Oven; beat these wel together and poure it to your Almonds, then butter your Plates and dust your Cakes with Sugar and Flower, and when they are a little brown, draw them, and when the oven is colder set them in again on browne Papers, and they will looke whiter.

Master Rudstones *Posset.*

Take a Pint of Sack, a quarter of a pint of Ale three quarters of a pound of Sugar, boyle all these well together, take two yolks of Eggs and sixteen whites very well beaten, put this to your boyling Sack & slice it very well together till it be thick on the coales; then take the three pints of Milk or Cream being boyled to a quart, it must stand and cool till the Eggs thicken, put it to your Sack and Eggs, and stir them well together, then cover it with a Plate and so serve it.

To boyle a Capon with Ranioles.

Take a good young Capon, trusse it and draw it to boyle, and parboyle it a little, then let it lye in fair Water being pickt very cleane and white, then boyle it in strong broth while it be enough, but first prepare your Ranioles as followeth; Take a good quantity of Beet leaves, and boyle them in Water very tender, then take them out, and get all the water very cleane out of them, then take six sweet breads of Veale, and boyle and mince them white, mince them small, and then boyl Herbs also, and four or five Marrow bones, break them and get all the Marrow out of them, and boyle the bigger peice of them in water by it selfe, and put the other into the minced Herbs, then take halfe a pound of Raisins of the Sun stoned, and mince them small, and halfe a pound of Dates the skin off, and mince them also, and a quarter of a pound of Pomecitron minced small, then take of Naples-bisket a good quantity, and put all these together on a Charger or a great Dish with halfe a pound of sweet Butter, and worke it together with your hands as you do a peice of Past, and season it with a little Nutmeg, Ginger, Cinamon, and Salt, & Permasan Cheese grated with hard Sugar grated also, then mingle all together well, and make a Past with the finest flower, six yolks of Eggs, a little Saffron beaten small, halfe a pound of sweet Butter, a little Salt, with some faire water hot (not boyling) and make up your Past, then drive out a long sheet of Past with an even Rowling Pin as thin as possible you can, and lay your ingredients in small heaps, round or long which you please in the Past, then cover them with the Past & cut them with a jag asunder and so make more or more till you have made two hundred or more, then have a good broad Pan or Kettle halfe full of strong Broth, boyling leisurely, and put in your Ransoles one by one, and let them boyle a quarter of an hour, then take up your Capon, lay it in a great Dish, and put one the Ransoles, & strew on them grated Cheese, Naples-Bisket grated, Cinamon and Sugar, then more and more Cinamon & Cheese, while you have filled your Dish; then put softly on melted Butter with a little strong Broth, your Marrow Pomecitron, Lemons sliced and serve it up, and so put it into the Dish so Ransoles may be part fryed with sweet but Clarified butter, either a quarter of them or halfe as you please; if the butter be not Clarified, it will spoile your Ransoles.

To make a Bisque of Carps.

Take twelve small Carps, and one great one, all Male Carps, draw them and take out all the Melts, flea the twelve small Carps, cut off their Heads and take out their Tongues and take the fish from the bones of the flead Carps, and twelve Oysters, two or three yelks of Hard eggs, mash altogether, season it with Cloves, Mace and Salt, and make thereof a stiffe searce, add thereto the yolks of foure or five Eggs to bind it, fashion that first into bals or Lopings as you please, lay them into a deep Dish or Earthen Pan, and put thereto twenty or thirty great Oysters, two or three Anchoves, the Milts and Tongues of your twelve Carps, halfe a pound of fresh butter, the Liquor of your Oysters, the juyce of a Lemon or two; a little White-wine some of Corbilion wherein your great Carpe is boyled, and a whole Onyon, so set them a stewing on a soft fire and make a hoop therewith; for the great Carp you must scald him and draw him, and lay him for half an hour with the other Carps Heads in a deep Pan with so much White wine Vinegar as will cover and serve to boyle him, and the other Heads in; put therein Pepper, whole Mace, a race of Ginger, Nutmeg, Salt sweet Herbs, an Onyon or two sliced, a Lemon; when you boyle your Carps, poure your Liquor with the Spice into the Kettle wherein you will boyle him; when it is boyled put in your Carp, let it not boyle too fast for breaking; after the Carp hath boyled a while put in the Head, when it is enough take off the Kettle, and let the Carps and the Heads keep warme in the Liquor till you goe to dish them. When you dresse your Bisque, take a large Silver dish, set it on the fire, lay therein Sippets of bread, then put in a Ladlefull of your Corbilion, then take up your great Carp and lay him in the midst of the Dish, then range the twelve heads about the Carp, then lay the searce of the Carp, lay that in, then your Oysters, Milts, and Tongues, then poure on the Liquor wherein the searce was boyled, wring in the juyce of a Lemon and two Oranges; Garnish your Dish with pickled Barberries, Lemons and Oranges, and serve it very hot to the Table.

To boyle a Pike and Eele together.

Take a quart of White-Wine and a pint and a halfe of White-Wine-Vinegar, two quarts of Water, and almost a pint of Salt, a handfull of Rosemary and Tyme; the Liquor must boyle before you put in your Fish and Herbs; the Eele with the skins must be put in a quarter of an hour before the Pike, with a little large Mace, and twenty cornes of Pepper.

To make an Outlandish dish.

Take the liver of a Hogg, and cut it in small pieces about the bigness of a span, then take Anni-seed, or French-seed, Pepper and Salt, and season them therewithall, and lay every piece severally round in the caule of the Hogg, and so roast them on a Bird-Spit.

To make a Portugall Dish.

Take the Guts, Gizards and Liver of two fat Capons, cut away the Galles from the Liver, and make clean the Gizards and put them into a Dish of clean water, slit the Gut as you do a Calves Chaldron but take off none of the fat, then lay the Guts about an hour in White-wine, as the Guts soke, half boyle Gizards and Livers, then take a long wooden broach, and spit your Gizards and Liver thereon, but not close one to another, then take and wipe the Guts somewhat dry in Cloth, and season them with Salt and beaten Pepper, Cloves and Mace, then wind the Guts upon the wooden Broach about the Liver, and Gizards, then tye the wooden Broach to spin, and lay them to the fire to roast, and roast them very brown, and bast them not at all till they be enough, then take the Gravy of Mutton, the juyce of two or three Oranges, and a grain of Saffron, mix all well together, and with a spoon bast your roast, let it drop into the same Dish. Then draw it, and serve it to the Table with the same sauce.

To dresse a dish of Hartichoaks.

Take and boyle them in the Beef-pot, when they are tender sodden, take off the tops, leaving the bottoms with some round about them, then put them into a Dish, put some fair water to them, two or three spoonfuls of Sack, a spoonfull of Sugar, and so let them boyle upon the Coales, still pouring on the Liquor to give it a good tast, when they have boyled halfe an hour take the Liquor from them, and make ready some Cream boyled and thickned with the yolk of an Egge or two, whole Mace, Salt, and Sugar with some lumps of marrow, boyle it in the Cream, when it is boyled put a good piece of sweet butter into it, and toast some toasts, and lay them under your Hartichoaks, and poure your Cream, and butter on them, Garnish it, &c.

To dresse a Fillet of Veale the Italian way. Take a young tender Fillet of Veale, pick away all the skins in the fold of the flesh, after you have picked it out clean, so that no skins are left, nor any hard thing; put to it some good White-Wine (that is not too sweet) in a bowl & wash it, & crush it well in the Wine; doe so twice, then strew upon it a powder that is called *Tamara* in *Italy*, and so much Salt as will season it well, mingle the Powder well upon the Pasts of your meat, then poure to it so much White-Wine as will cover it when it is thrust down into a narrow Pan; lay a Trencher on it and a weight to keep it downe, let it lye two nights and one day, put a little Pepper to it when you lay it in the Sauce, and after it it is sowsed so long, take it out and put it into a Pipkin with some good Beef-broth, but you must not take any of the pickle to it, but onely Beef-broth that is sweet and not salt; cover it close and set it on the Embers, onely put into it with the Broth a few whole Cloves and Mace, and let it stew till it be enough. It will be very tender and of an excellent Taste; it must be served with the same broth as much as will cover it.

To make the Italian, take Coriander seed two Ounces, Aniseed one ounce, Fennel-seed one ounce, Cloves two ounces, Cinamon one ounce; These must be beaten into a grosse powder, putting into it a little powder of Winter-savoury; if you like it, keep this in a Vial-glasse close stopt for your use.

To dresse Soales.

Take a Pair of Soales, lard them through with watered fresh Salmon, then lay your Soales on a Table, or Pie-plate, cut your Salmon, lard all of an equal length on each side, and leave the Lard but short, then flower the Soales, and fry them in the best Ale you can get; when they are fryed lay them in a warme Pie-plate, and so serve them to the Table with a Sallet dish full of Anchovy sauce, and three or four Oranges.

To make Furmity.

Take a quart of Creame, a quarter of a pound of French-barley the whitest you can get, and boyle it very tender in three or four severall waters, and let it be cold, then put both together, put in it a blade of Mace, a Nutmeg cut in quarters, a race of Ginger cut in three or five pieces, and so let it boyle a good while, still stirring, and season it with Sugar to your tast, then take the yolks of four Eggs and beat them with a little Cream, and stir them into it, and so let it boyle a little after the Egs are in, then have ready blanched and beaten twenty Almonds kept from oyling, with a little Rosewater, then take a boulter, strainer, and rub your Almonds with a little of your Furmity through the strainer, but set on the fire no more, and stir in a little Salt and a little sliced Nutmeg, pickt out of the great peices of it, and put it in a dish, and serve it.

To make Patis, or Cabbage Cream.

Take thirty Ale pints of new milke, and set it on the fire in a Kettle till it be scalding hot, stirring it oft to keep it from creaming, then put in forth, into thirty Pans of Earth, as you put it forth, take off the bubbles with a spoon, let it stand till it be cold, then take off the Cream with two such slices as you beat Bisket bread with, but they must be very thin and not too broad, then when the Milk is dropped off the Cream, you must lay it upon a Pye-plate, you must scour the Kettle very clean and heat the Milk again, and so four or five times. In the lay of it, first lay a stalk in the midst of the Plate, let the rest of the Cream be laid upon that sloping, between every laying you must scrape Sugar and sprinkle Rosewater, and if you will, the powder of Musk, and Ambergreece, in the heating of the Milk be carefull of smoak.

To make Pap.

Take three quarts of new milk, set it on the fire in a dry silver Dish, or Bason, when it begins to boyle skim it, then put thereto a handfull of flour & yolks of three Eggs, which you must have well mingled together with a Ladlefull of cold Milk, before you put it to the Milk that boyles, and as it boyles, stir it all the while till it be enough, and in the boyling, season it with a little Salt, and a little fine beaten Sugar and so keeping it stirred till it be boyled as thick as you desire, then put it forth into another Dish and serve it up.

To make Spanish Pap.

Take three spoonfuls of Rice-floure, finely beaten and searced, two yolks of Eggs, three spoonfuls of Sugar, three or foure spoonfuls of Rosewater. Temper these fouer together, then put them to a pint of cold Cream, then set it on the fire and keep it stirred till it come to a reasonable thicknesse, then Dish it and serve it up.

To poach eggs.

Take a dozen of new laid Eggs and flesh of foure or five Partridges, or other; mince it so small as you can season it with a few beaten Cloves, Mace, and Nutmeg, into a Silver Dish, with a Ladlefull or two of the Gravy of Mutton, wherein two or three Anchoves are dissolved; then set it a stewing on a fire of Char-Coales, and after it is halfe stewed, as it boyles, break in your Eggs, one by one, and as you break them, poure away most part of the Whites, and with one end of your Egg-shell, make a place in your Dish of meat, and therein put your Yolks of your Eggs, round in order amongst your meat, and so let them stew till your Eggs be enough, then grate in a little Nutmeg, and the juyce of a couple of Oranges; have a care none of the Seeds goe in, wipe your Dish and garnish your Dish, with four or five whole Onions,&c.

A Pottage of Beef Pallats.

Take Beefe Pallats after they be boyled tender in the Beefe Kettle, or Pot among some other meat, blanch and serve them cleane, then cut each Pallat in two, and set them a stewing between two Dishes with a piece of leer Bacon, an handful of Champignions, five or six sweetbreads of Veale, a Ladlefull or two of strong broth, and as much gravy of Mutton, an Onion or two, five or six Cloves, and a blade or two of Mace, and a piece of Orange Pils; as your Pallats stew, make ready your Dish with the bottoms and tops of two or three Cheat Loaves dryed and moystned with some Gravy of Mutton, and the broth your Palats stew in, you must have the Marrow of two or three beef-bones stewed in a little broth between two Dishes in great pieces; when your Pallats and Marrow iss stewed, and you ready to Dish it, take out all the Spices, Onyon and Bacon, and lay it in your Plates, sweetbread, and Champigneons, pour in the Broath they were stewed in & lay on your peices of Marrow, wring the juyce of two or three Oranges; and so serve it to the Table very hot.

The Jacobins Pottage.

Take the flesh of a washed Capon or Turkey cold, mince it so small as you can, then grate or scrape among the flesh two or three ounces of Parmasants or old Holland Cheese, season it with beaten Cloves, Nutmeg, Mace, and Salt, then take the bottoms and tops of foure or five new Rowles, dry them before the fire, or in an Oven, then put them into a faire silver Dish set it upon the fire, wet your bread in a Ladle full of strong Broth, and a Ladlefull of Gravy of Mutton then strow on your minced meat all of an equall thicknesse in each place, then stick twelve or eighteen peices of Marrow as bigge as Walnuts, and pour on an handfull of pure Gravy of Mutton then cover your Dish close, and as it stews adde now and then some Gravy of Mutton there to, thrust your Knife sometimes to the bottome, to keep the bread from sticking to the Dish, let it so stew stil, till you are ready to Dish it away, and when you serve it, if need require, ad more Gravy of Mutton, wring the juyce of two or three Oranges, wipe your Dishes brims, and serve it to the Table in the same Dish.

To Salt a Goose.

Take a fat Goose and bone him, but leave the brest bone, wipe him with a clean cloath, then salt him one fortnight, then hang him up for one fortnight or three weeks, then boyl him in running water very tender, and serve him with Bayleaves.

A way of stewing Chickens or Rabbets.

Take two three or foure Chickens, and let them be about the bigness of a Partridge, boyl them til they be half boyled enough, then take them off and cut them into little peices, putting the joynt bone one from another, and let not the meat be minced, but cut into great bits, not so exactly but more or lesse, the brest bones are not so proper to be put in, but put the meat together with the other bones (upon which there must also be some meat remaining) into a good quantity of that Water or Broth wherein the Chickens were boyled, and set it then over a Chaffing-Dish of coales betweeen two Dishes, that so it may stew on till it be fully enough; but first season it with Salt and gross Pepper, and afterwards add Oyl to it, more or lesse according to the goodnesse thereof; and a little before you take it from the fire, you must adde such a quantity of juyce of Lemons as may best agree with your Taste. This makes an excellent dish of Meat, which must be served up in the Liquor; and though for a need it may be made with Butter instead of Oyl, and with Vinegar in stead of Juyce of Lemons, yet is the other incomparably better for such as are not Enemies to Oyle. The same Dish may be made also of Veal, or Partridge, or Rabbets, and indeed the best of them all, is Rabbets, if they be used so before Michaelmas, for afterwards me-thinkes they grow ranke; for though they be fatter, yet the flesh is more hard and dry.

A Pottage of Capons.

Take a couple of young Capons, Trusse and set them and fill their bellies with Marrow, put them into a Pipkin with a knuckle of Veale, a Neck of Mutton, and a Marrow bone, and some sweet bread of Veale; season your Broth with Cloves, Mace, and a little Salt, set it to the fire, and let it boyle gently till your Capons be enough, but boyle them not too much; as your Capons boyle, make ready the bottomes and Tops of eight or ten new Rowles, and put them dryed into a faire Silver Dish wherein you serve the Capons; set it on the fire, and put to your bread, two Ladlefuls of Broth wherein your Capons are boyled and a Ladlefull of the Gravy of Mutton; so cover your Dish, and let it stand till you Dish up yovr Capons if need require, adde now and then a Ladlefull of Broth and Gravy, least the bread grow dry; when you are ready to serve it, first lay in the Marrow bone, then the Capons on each side, then fill up your Dish with the Gravy of Mutton, wherein you must wring the juyce of a Lemon or two, then with a spoon take off all the fat that swimmeth on the pottage, then garnish your Capon with the sweet Breads and some Lemons, and so serve it.

To dresse Soales another way.

Take Soales, fry them halfe enough, then take Wine seasoned with Salt, grated Ginger, and a little Garlick, let the Wine, and seasoning boyle in a Dish, when that boyles and your Soales are halfe fry'd, take the Soales and put them into the Wine, when they are sufficiently stewed, upon their backs, lay the two halfs open on the one side and on the other, then lay Anchoves finely washed along, and on the sides over again, let them stew till they be ready to be eaten, then take them out, lay them on the Dish, pour some of the clear Liquor which they stew in upon them, and squeeze an Orange in.

A Carpe Pye.

Take Carps scald them, take out the great bones, pound the Carps in a stone Morter pound some of the blood with the flesh which must be at the discretion of the Cook because it must not be too soft, then lard it with the belly of a very fat Eale, season it, and bake it like red Deere and eat it cold.

This is meat for a Pope.

To boyle Ducks after the french fashion.

Take and lard them and put them upon a spit, and halfe roast them, then draw them & put them into a Pipkin, and put a quart of Clarit Wine into it, and Chesnuts, & a pint of great Oysters taking the beards from them, and three Onyons minced very small, some Mace and a little beaten Ginger, a little Tyme stript, a Crust of a French Rowle grated put into it to thicken it, and so dish it upon sops. This may be diversified, if there be strong broth there need not be so much Wine put in, and if there be no oysters or Chesnuts you may put in Hartichoak bottoms, Turnips, Colliflowers, Bacon in thin slices, Sweet bread's, &c.

To boyle a Goose with Sausages.

Take your Goose and salt it two or three dayes, then trusse it to boyle, cut Lard as big as the top of your finger, as much as will Lard the flesh of the brest, season your lard with Pepper, Mace, and Salt; put it a boyling in Beefe broth if you have any, or water, season your Liquor with a little Salt, and Pepper grosly beaten an ounce or two, a bundle of Bayleaves, Rosemary and Tyme, tyed altogether; you must have prepared your Cabbage or sausages boyl'd very tender, squeese all the water from them, then put them into a Pipkin, put to them a little strong broth or Claret Wine, an Onyon or two; season it with Pepper, Salt and Mace to your tast; six Anchoves dissolved, put altogether, and let them stew a good while on the fire; put a Ladle of thicke Butter, a little Vinegar, when your Goose is boyled enough, and your Cabbage on Sippets of bread and the Goose on the

them close one to another; I seldome lay any in Hay, I turne and rub them with a rotten cloth especially when they are old, once a week least they rot.

To Pickle Purslaine.

Take Purslaine, stalks and all, boyl them tender in faire Water, then lay them drying upon linning Cloaths, then being dryed, put them into the Galley-pots and cover them with wine Vinegar mixt with Salt, and not make the Pickle so strong as for Cucumbers.

FINIS.